WOMEN'S
WORLD CUP HEROES

BY THOMAS CAROTHERS

SUPER SOCCER

SportsZone

An Imprint of Abdo Publishing
abdobooks.com

abdobooks.com

Published by Abdo Publishing, a division of ABDO, PO Box 398166, Minneapolis, Minnesota 55439. Copyright © 2019 by Abdo Consulting Group, Inc. International copyrights reserved in all countries. No part of this book may be reproduced in any form without written permission from the publisher. SportsZone™ is a trademark and logo of Abdo Publishing.

Printed in the United States of America, North Mankato, Minnesota
092018
012019

Cover Photos: Carmen Jaspersen/picture-alliance/dpa/AP Images, foreground; Shutterstock Images, ball
Interior Photos: Shutterstock Images, 1; Lacy Atkins/The San Francisco Examiner/AP Images, 5; Eric Risberg/AP Images, 7; Mark J. Terrill/AP Images, 8, 19; Tommy Cheng/AFP/Getty Images, 10–11, 13; Ben Radford/Getty Images Sport/Getty Images, 14–15; Rick Bowmer/AP Images, 16; Petr David Josek/AP Images, 21; Patrik Stollarz/AFP/Getty Images, 22; Julian Avram/Cal Sport Media/AP Images, 25; Elaine Thompson/AP Images, 26; Xinhua/Imago/Icon Sportswire, 29

Editor: Bradley Cole
Series Designer: Laura Polzin

Library of Congress Control Number: 2018949086

Publisher's Cataloging-in-Publication Data

Names: Carothers, Thomas, author.
Title: Women's World Cup heroes / by Thomas Carothers.
Description: Minneapolis, Minnesota : Abdo Publishing, 2019 | Series: Super soccer | Includes online resources and index.
Identifiers: ISBN 9781532117473 (lib. bdg.) | ISBN 9781641856294 (pbk) | ISBN 9781532170331 (ebook)
Subjects: LCSH: FIFA Women's World Cup--Juvenile literature. | Soccer--Juvenile literature. | Soccer for women--Juvenile literature. | Soccer players--Juvenile literature.
Classification: DDC 796.3346--dc23

★TABLE OF★ CONTENTS

CHAPTER 1

CHASTAIN'S CLASSIC KICK

I t was a game that had already lived up to its billing. The United States Women's National Team (USWNT) and China had battled to a 0–0 draw through 90 minutes of regulation and another half hour of extra time.

After 120 minutes of give-and-take between the teams, the record crowd of 90,185 at the Rose Bowl in Pasadena, California, was at a fever pitch. Only a shootout would settle it. The team with the most successful penalty kicks after five rounds would be the winner of the 1999 Women's World Cup.

Both the United States and China scored in the first two rounds. Carla Overbeck and Joy Fawcett beat Chinese goalkeeper Gao Hong. Xie Huilin and Qiu Haiyan both scored against American keeper Briana Scurry.

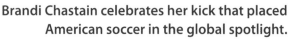

Brandi Chastain celebrates her kick that placed American soccer in the global spotlight.

But the game was about to be turned on its head in the third round. Scurry dove to her left and saved Liu Yang's attempt. Now the United States had the advantage. If the Americans made their final three penalty kicks, the championship was theirs.

BRIANA SCURRY

Before Hope Solo, there was Briana Scurry. Scurry was the original superstar goalkeeper for the USWNT. A native of Minneapolis, Minnesota, Scurry played for the United States from 1994 to 2008. She won gold medals with Team USA in 1996 and 2008. Her save of Liu Ying's penalty attempt in the 1999 Women's World Cup helped lead to Brandi Chastain's eventual game-winning kick. In 2017 Scurry became the first black woman elected to the US National Soccer Hall of Fame.

Kristine Lilly and Mia Hamm both made their kicks, as did China's Zhang Ouying and Sun Wen. That meant the entire game landed on the shoulders of Brandi Chastain.

The California native was just weeks away from her 31st birthday. Chastain had been a part of the USWNT since 1988. She was part of the squad that had defeated China to win the 1996 Olympic gold medal. Now, three years later, result of the Women's World Cup was up to her.

American goalkeeper Briana Scurry makes a save to set up Chastain's final kick.

Chastain lined up the kick in front of thousands of US supporters clad in red, white, and blue. Behind her, players from both sides stood arm-in-arm with their teammates as they awaited the kick.

Gao stood 12 yards (11 m) away, staring down Chastain as the American backed away from the ball, preparing to make the kick. Then Chastain ran up to the ball and fired with her left foot.

Chastain's kick in front of an American crowd set off a wave of support for women's soccer in the United States.

The ball sailed toward the upper right corner of the net. Chastain's aim was true—the only question was whether Gao could make the save. Gao guessed correctly and dove to meet the ball. But the ball carried past her outstretched arms and into the net. The United States had won.

As her teammates sprinted to her, Chastain ripped off her jersey and fell to her knees. She pumped her fists in the air. That pose became a timeless image of women's soccer. It would be copied by many players for years after.

Chastain rose to her feet to embrace teammates. They surrounded her in celebration as the United States claimed the Women's World Cup championship in front of its home crowd. Chastain became a worldwide celebrity, and the image of her game-winning celebration graced the covers of *Sports Illustrated*, *Newsweek*, and *Time* magazines, to name just a few.

The game, the celebration, and the win were game changers for women's soccer in the United States, inspiring children throughout the country. Some of those children who watched the game that day, including Alex Morgan, would go on to play for the USWNT. They would win their own Women's World Cup and Olympic championships, just like Chastain.

CHAPTER 2

AMERICAN PIONEERS

The first-ever Women's World Cup occurred eight years earlier and an ocean away from southern California. The women who played in the tournament gained far less attention than in 1999 and a fraction of the fame the USWNT knows today. However, the championship earned by that first Women's World Cup winner in 1991 was no less historic.

The Americans had come a long way since the team's first match in against Denmark during a 1985 tournament in Italy. By 1991 it was on a level playing field with the rest of the world and headed to China with confidence.

Twelve teams competed in that first Women's World Cup. They were spread out in three groups, with the Americans in Group B. The USWNT met one of its toughest tests of the

US forward Carin Jennings (12) makes a move in a group play match against Sweden.

tournament in its first game. The United States faced Sweden, a team that would become one of the Americans' fiercest rivals.

The United States won 3–2 with 19-year-old Mia Hamm scoring the final goal. Two young players joined Hamm in the American midfield, 20-year-olds Kristine Lilly and Julie Foudy. Their speed and attack style overwhelmed other teams. It formed the foundation for success for the rest of the decade.

After allowing two goals in its first game, the United States did not allow another goal through its next three games. The Americans shut out Brazil and Japan to win Group B. Behind five goals by Michelle Akers, the USWNT blew out Chinese Taipei 7–0 in the quarterfinals. Next up for the Americans was a semifinal game against Germany. Carin Jennings scored three goals. The United States rolled into the Women's World Cup final with a 5–2 win.

The Americans faced Norway in front of 63,000 fans, and the event was televised around the world. This game gave birth to the rivalry between the teams. The USWNT and Norway would battle for dominance for the next decade. The United States took the lead 20 minutes into the game on an Akers

From left, Julie Foudy, Michelle Akers, and Carin Jennings celebrate the US victory in the first Women's World Cup.

header goal. Norway answered with its own nine minutes later. The game remained tied until the 78th minute.

Then Akers struck again. She corralled a long pass and beat two defenders and the keeper to tap the ball into the net. The goal gave the USWNT a 2–1 win. And the United States was the first Women's World Cup champion.

CHAPTER 3

GERMANY TOPS SWEDEN

The first three Women's World Cup championships were the lone property of the United States and Norway. The Americans earned two titles, and Norway had one.

Norway's Women's World Cup win came at Germany's expense. The Norwegians defeated the Germans 2–0 in the 1995 Women's World Cup final. Germany finished fourth in 1991 and bowed out of the tournament in the quarterfinals in 1999. While the German men's team had been a world power for decades, Germany's women had yet to make their mark at the top level. That all changed in 2003.

The United States hosted its second consecutive Women's World Cup that year. The tournament had originally been scheduled to return to China. But an outbreak of a potentially

Birgit Prinz, *right*, dribbles past Russian midfielder Tatiana Skotnikova in the quarterfinals.

Germany scored the first goal of the match off a header by
Kerstin Garefrakes (18).

deadly virus in China that summer forced the tournament to
move to the United States.

Germany powered through its group stage games, winning
all three games. The Germans outscored the opposition 13–2.
Then Germany destroyed Russia 7–1 in its quarterfinal game.

It advanced to face tournament host and defending Women's World Cup champion the United States in the semifinals.

The United States had also dominated its group with a 3–0 record before shutting out Norway 1–0 in its quarterfinal game. Nearly 28,000 fans were on hand in Portland, Oregon, to watch Germany and the United States on October 5.

Kerstin Garefrakes gave the Germans a 1–0 lead in the 15th minute. It proved to be the game winner. Germany added two more late goals to win 3–0 and advance to the final for the first time since 1995.

Sweden, a 2–1 winner over Canada in the other semifinal, met Germany in the final. This meant the 2003 Women's World Cup champion would be a

SCHEDULING SHAKEUP

The 2003 Women's World Cup had to be moved from China to the United States due to the SARS epidemic in China. SARS is a serious form of pneumonia that broke out in the country that year. Fédération Internationale de Football Association (FIFA) decided to move the Women's World Cup to the United States in May 2003, just under four months before it was to begin. China was awarded hosting of the 2007 Women's World Cup to make up for losing the 2003 tournament.

first-time winner. The game was played in front of 26,137 fans in the new home of the Major League Soccer's Los Angeles Galaxy, the Home Depot Center in suburban Carson, California.

Sweden struck first when Hanna Ljungberg split a pair of German defenders, leaving her all alone on goalkeeper Silke Rottenberg. Ljungberg slotted the ball home under a diving Rottenberg and into the goal to give Sweden a 1–0 lead just before halftime.

The advantage did not last long. On the initial German attack of the second half, Maren Meinert blasted the ball under Swedish keeper Caroline Jonsson to knot the score at 1–1. Germany's goal came less than a minute after play restarted, setting the stage for an exciting finish.

Neither team scored in the remainder of the second half. The contest went to extra time to decide the Women's World Cup champion.

Eight minutes into added time, Nia Kuenzer leaped high above the Swedish defense on a free kick and headed the ball over Jonsson for the game-winning goal. The sudden-death

Germany's players celebrate after Nia Kuenzer's golden goal gave them a 2–1 Women's World Cup final win over Sweden.

overtime immediately ended with what is called a "golden goal" in favor of the ecstatic German team.

It was the last time a Women's World Cup was decided by a sudden-death goal. The rules were changed the following year to allow for the full two 15-minute periods of added extra time to be played out regardless of whether either team scores.

Germany joined the United States and Norway as the only Women's World Cup champions to date. Four years later, the Germans became the first nation to win back-to-back titles by defeating Brazil 2–0 in the 2007 final in China.

CHAPTER 4

JAPAN STUNS WORLD

Japan started off the 2011 tournament with strong performances through group play. With two wins and one loss in Group B, Japan qualified for the knockout round.

Heading into 2011 Japan had won only three of its previous 16 Women's World Cup games. Japan's lone appearance in the knockout round ended with a 4–0 loss to the USWNT squad in the 1995 quarterfinals.

But 2011 was a new chance for the Japanese, who were No. 4 in the world rankings as they entered the Women's World Cup. After winning two group matches for the first time in its Women's World Cup history, Japan made even more history by knocking off the host country and defending champion Germany 1–0 in extra time on a goal by Karina Maruyama.

Japan's Homare Sawa celebrates her goal that helped her team beat Sweden 3–1.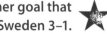

US keeper Hope Solo couldn't stop Saki Kumagai's kick, giving Japan the victory.

Japan was not finished there. Up next was a 3–1 defeat of Sweden in the semifinal round. Sweden seized an early 1–0 lead. Then Japan rallied back with a pair of goals by Nahomi Kawasumi and a score by captain Homare Sawa.

The victory advanced Japan to a Women's World Cup final meeting against an American team that was determined to reclaim the title it last held in 1999.

The Americans were the top-ranked team in the world entering the tournament. However, they were inconsistent. The United States lost to Sweden in group play and was nearly defeated in the quarterfinals by Brazil.

Japan and the United States faced off in front of 48,817 fans in Frankfurt, Germany. The Americans took the lead twice, only to see the Japanese battle back both times. The first time Alex Morgan put the Americans up 1–0 in the 69th minute. She sent a screamer into the net past Japanese keeper Ayumi Kaihori after receiving a long pass from teammate Megan Rapinoe. Japan and the United States both missed several scoring opportunities. But then Aya Miyama intercepted a pass in front of the American goal and sent the ball past American goalkeeper Hope Solo. The score was 1–1 in the 81st minute.

The game went into extra time, during which Abby Wambach put her team back out in front 2–1 in the 104th minute. But Sawa tied the game with a deflected goal off a corner kick with less than three minutes to play.

A 2–2 tie sent the game into penalty kicks. The US players missed on their first three tries. Japan made two of its three attempts. Wambach beat Kaihori. It came down to Saki Kumagai. She looked up and then sent the ball rocketing past a diving Solo and into the net. The goal completed Japan's journey from underdog to Women's World Cup champion.

CHAPTER 5

WAMBACH GOES OUT A WINNER

The USWNT stewed for four years over its loss to Japan in 2011. It had also been 16 years since Brandi Chastain ripped off her jersey to celebrate the United States' last Women's World Cup title. The Americans were hungry to return to the top spot. The last time the United States won the Women's World Cup, Abby Wambach was still two years away from being named to the United States' roster.

Now, Wambach was playing in her last of four Women's World Cups. She had won two Olympic gold medals with the USWNT, including the defeat of Japan in the 2012 London Games. However, a Women's World Cup title had evaded her, and at 35 years old, she knew the 2015 tournament in Canada was her last chance.

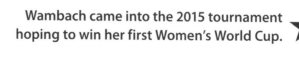

Wambach came into the 2015 tournament hoping to win her first Women's World Cup.

From left, Megan Rapinoe, Lauren Holiday, and Carli Lloyd celebrate during the Women's World Cup final.

The United States went undefeated through group play with two wins and one draw to win Group D. However, Japan, carrying the swagger of a defending Women's World Cup champion, went 3–0 to win Group C.

The knockout stage was tense for both teams. As it had done in the group stage, Japan won all three games against the Netherlands, Australia, and England by a single goal. The Americans did not allow a goal in any of their knockout games. The United States defeated Colombia 2–0, China 1–0, and Germany 2–0. The Americans had given up just one goal in the entire tournament, to Australia in the opening game. They won 3–1.

But while the Americans' defense had been dominant, the offense had not been overwhelming. Many expected the 2015 Women's World Cup final to be a close, low-scoring matchup. It could not have gone much differently.

Whereas the United States missed several early opportunities to score on Japan in the 2011 Women's World Cup, the USWNT overwhelmed Japan in front of 53,341 fans at BC Place in Vancouver, British Columbia. It took just three minutes for the United States to take a lead it did not relinquish. Carli Lloyd sprinted into the box unmarked on an American corner kick and swiftly deposited the ball into the back of the net to put her team up 1–0.

Two minutes later, it was Lloyd again. The US captain found the ball on her foot after it bounced around the Japanese penalty box following a free kick. Lloyd tapped the ball through a pair of defenders and past goalkeeper Ayumi Kaihori to put the Americans up 2–0 just five minutes into the contest.

In the 14th minute, a failed clearance from the Japanese defense landed the ball on Lauren Holiday's right foot directly in front of the goal. Holiday fired a shot into the net, and it was USA 3, Japan 0.

The blitz continued. Two minutes later Lloyd caught Kaihori far out of her goal and launched a shot from the halfway line. It sailed over the Japanese keeper and into the goal for a 4–0 American lead, just 16 minutes into the game. Thousands of USWNT fans were already well on their way to celebrating a United States victory with 70-plus minutes left to play.

Japan gave America a bit of pause by drawing to within 4–2 early in the second half. However, a final American goal by Tobin Heath in the 54th minute finished off what became a 5–2 win for the United States.

Wambach subbed on for her final Women's World Cup appearance in the 79th minute and was on the field as the USWNT celebrated becoming the first team to win three

The Americans celebrated bringing home their third Women's World Cup, the first since 1999.

Women's World Cup championships. Lloyd tied for the Women's World Cup's top scorer, as her three goals in the final gave her six for the tournament. She also earned the Golden Ball award as the Women's World Cup's top player. Solo won the Golden Glove as the tournament's best keeper for the second consecutive Women's World Cup.

GLOSSARY

extra time

Two 15-minute periods added to a game if the score is tied at the end of regulation.

forward

Also called a striker, the player who plays nearest the opponent's goal.

goalkeeper

A player whose primary duty is to prevent the ball from entering the net.

group stage

The part of a tournament when teams are divided into smaller groups or pools; each team faces the others in group, and those with the best records move on to the knockout stage.

knockout stage

A stage in a competition in which one loss eliminates a team.

midfielder

A player who stays mostly in the middle third of the field and links the defenders with the forwards.

penalty box

The area in front of the goal where a player is granted a penalty kick if he or she is fouled.

penalty kick

A play in which a shooter faces a goalkeeper alone; it is used to decide tie games or as a result of the foul.

subbed on

When a player is brought into the game as a substitute for another player who is leaving the pitch.

MORE INFORMATION

BOOKS

Jökulsson, Illugi. *Alex Morgan.* New York: Abbeville, 2015.

Jökulsson, Illugi. *Stars of Women's Soccer.* New York: Abbeville, 2018.

Marquardt, Meg. *STEM in Soccer.* Minneapolis, MN: Abdo Publishing, 2018.

ONLINE RESOURCES

Booklinks
NONFICTION NETWORK
FREE! ONLINE NONFICTION RESOURCES

To learn more about the Women's World Cup, visit **abdobooklinks.com**. These links are routinely monitored and updated to provide the most current information available.

INDEX

ABOUT THE AUTHOR

Thomas Carothers has been a sportswriter for the past 15 years in the Minneapolis–St. Paul area in Minnesota. He has worked for a number of print and online publications, mostly focusing on prep sports coverage. He lives in Minneapolis with his wife and a house full of dogs.